ICE HOCKEY LEGENDS

Wayne Gretzky

Brett Hull

Jaromir Jagr

Mario Lemieux

Eric Lindros

Mark Messier

CHELSEA HOUSE PUBLISHERS

ICE HOCKEY LEGENDS

WAYNE GRETZKY

Josh Wilker

CHELSEA HOUSE PUBLISHERS
Philadelphia

Produced by Daniel Bial and Associates
New York, New York

Picture research by Alan Gottlieb
Cover illustration by Bill Vann

First Printing

1 3 5 7 9 8 6 4 2

Library of Congress Cataloging-in-Publication Data

Wilker, Josh.
        Wayne Gretzky / Josh Wilker.
            p.   cm. — (Ice hockey legends)
        Includes bibliographical references (p.) and index.
        Summary: An account of the famous Edmonton Oiler and his ability
    that shattered every major single season scoring mark in the NHL
    record book.
        ISBN 0-7910-4554-4
        1. Gretzky, Wayne, 1961–   — Juvenile literature. 2. Hockey
    players—Canada—Biography—Juvenile literature. [1. Gretzky,
    Wayne, 1961–   . 2. Hockey players.] I. Title. II. Series.
    GV848.5.G73W55   1997
    796.962'092–dc21
        [b]   97-27362
                                                                    CIP
                                                                    AC

CONTENTS

CHAPTER 1
SEEING ALL OF EVERYTHING   7

CHAPTER 2
"YOU CAN'T BE NORMAL   15

CHAPTER 3
"THAT DARN KID HAS FUN"   23

CHAPTER 4
TEARING UP THE LEAGUE   31

CHAPTER 5
A TEAM ON THE RISE   37

CHAPTER 6
THE CHAMPION   45

CHAPTER 7
THE GAME STILL GIVES
ME JOY   55

STATISTICS   61
CHRONOLOGY   62
FURTHER READING   63
INDEX   64

SEEING ALL
OF EVERYTHING

The Edmonton Oilers took the ice at the start of the 1983-84 National Hockey League (NHL) season like a blue, white, and orange hurricane. The pucks flew at the goal from every direction. Right winger Jarri Kurri would finish the year with 52 goals. Left winger Glenn Anderson tallied 54. Defenseman Paul Coffey blasted in 40 goals, and Mark Messier, the ferocious Oilers left wing, struck for 37.

But none of these All-Star players commanded the primary attention of the often shell-shocked teams of the league. The Oilers were a hurricane, and the near-impossible task of the opposing team's defense was to snuff out the eye of this furious storm. It was no secret that the player who wore number 99 was the center of the Edmonton Oilers attack. "Everything that happens when he's on the ice revolves around him," said New York Islanders General Manag-

Wayne Gretzky has perhaps the greatest vision on ice—the ability to see all the action taking place and know where the puck is going next.

Gretzky unleashes a slapshot. He has uncanny precision in his shot, even while skating at top speed.

er Bill Torrey. On most nights, however, the eye of the storm could barely even be located, let alone snuffed, until it was much too late. When defeated players and coaches spoke afterward of the player that beat them, they often sounded like the survivors of a natural catastrophe.

"He's worse than Bobby Orr," said Philadelphia Flyers center Bobby Clarke, invoking the name of the player who had previously been most often mentioned as the best ever to lace up skates. "At least Orr started in his own end and you could brace yourself." Clarke, nearing the end of a Hall-of-Fame career of his own, had never opposed anyone like the Edmonton Oilers center. Said Clarke, "Gretzky just materializes out of nowhere."

At the start of the 1983-84 season, Wayne Gretzky was only 22 years old. Yet he had already shattered every major single-season scoring mark in the NHL record book. He was not big. He was not fast. He was not strong. His tepid shot on goal was most aptly described by goalie Chico Resch, who said, "You could wear driving gloves and catch one of his shots, and it wouldn't hurt." With his slight build and his delicate facial features he looked, when out of uniform, more like a cheerful, teenaged cashier at a supermarket than a professional athlete. Yet in only four seasons in the NHL he had completely eclipsed the records of such hockey legends as Orr, Maurice "Rocket" Richard, and Phil Esposito.

All-Star goalie Mike Liut lamented, "I'd direct a rebound into the corner and he'd be there waiting for it—*bang,* right back at me. It was like he knew where I was going to send the puck before *I* did. How does he do that?" Chico Resch also found himself asking questions when the subject of Wayne Gretzky came up. "What I want to know," he said, "is how did he always know what the toughest play would be for the goalie to make?"

"He looks out at the whole rink and can see all of everything," said Gretzky's linemate Jarri Kurri, "even into my head." Even into the future, according to a supremely qualified observer named Bobby Orr. Orr said of Gretzky, "He can see the whole ice surface. He doesn't hesitate. He's five, 10 seconds ahead of everyone else."

This uncanny prescience allowed Gretzky to control games. He knew where everyone on the ice was going to be at any given moment, and he used this knowledge to make the perfect pass to a streaking teammate, to locate the weak spot of a defense and go there and take a pass and score, or—and this was, for opponents, the most frustrating aspect of his game—to deftly elude steamrolling defenders who desired to crumple him against the boards. Said Boston Bruins General Manager Harry Sinden of the man who seemed to have eyes in the back of his head, "How are you going to body check him? I've never seen him hit yet. It's been said that the only way to do this might be when he's standing still singing the national anthem." Minnesota North Stars General Manager Lou Nanne added, "You can't hit Gretzky with a handful of confetti."

In his first four years in the league, only one team had found even partial success at slowing Gretzky down. The New York Islanders had done so while capturing the 1982-83 league championship—the fourth straight time the team from Long Island got their mitts on the hallowed Stanley Cup trophy. The Islanders had drubbed the high-flying Oilers in the finals, sweeping them in four games, and had somehow kept Wayne Gretzky from scoring a single goal. This humiliating setback did not sit well with Gretzky. "All summer I kept telling myself," he said, "'This has to be my year.'"

Gretzky had been awarded the league's most valuable player award in each of his first four years in the league. It was hard to imagine him getting any better. Yet as the 1983-84 season opened, Gretzky seemed to have added something to his game. He had always wanted to win,

but now that desire had ripened to an unstoppable hunger. He wanted the Stanley Cup. The Oilers blew away Washington 11-3, Pittsburgh 7-3, Winnipeg 8-4, and Quebec 7-4, and against New Jersey, Gretzky scoring three goals and dishing out five assists, the Oilers romped, 13-4.

Gretzky scored points (awarded for either a goal or an assist) in every one of the Oilers' first 30 games, matching the league consecutive-games scoring record he had established the previous year. He broke that record the following game and in the game after that he broke the record again. As the streak reached 40 games it began to capture the imagination of people not usually interested in hockey. Members of the media began comparing the streak to Joe DiMaggio's famous 56-game hitting streak in baseball.

Gretzky is slowed down for a moment as he is hooked by Ken Morrow of the New York Islanders. In this 1983 game, Gretzky scored his 300th goal and set an NHL record by scoring a point in his 31st consecutive game.

The two streaks, according to Oilers coach Glen Sather, were "very comparable from the historical point of their being so much more than what anyone else in either sport ever did."

In game 41, Gretzky poured in four goals and got four assists in the first two periods alone. In game 42 he scored three more goals. In game 43, while the Oilers were outnumbered on the ice for a Detroit Red Wings power play, Gretzky swiped the puck from Red Wings center Steve Yzerman and snapped a 25-foot wrist shot past the Red Wings' goalie. He scored again in the second period and, 29 seconds after that score, assisted on a goal by Wally Lindstrom. "Gretzky doesn't just make a good pass," said Lindstrom. "He makes the perfect pass."

Against Chicago, the streak appeared to be over. With 32 seconds left, and the Oilers clinging to a 4-3 lead, the Blackhawks pulled their goalie for an extra attacker. Gretzky had yet to score a point. The seconds slipped off the clock. With but seven ticks left, Blackhawks center Troy Murray controlled the puck. Gretzky saw into his mind. When Murray attempted a pass to teammate Doug Wilson, Gretzky was there. He knocked the puck into the air with his stick, slapped it down to the ice with his left hand, and, while warding off Murray from behind, he eased a shot into the empty net with two seconds left on the clock.

The streak kept going. "The pressure to get a point every night is beginning to bother me a little," said Gretzky after game 49. This was not the only thing bothering him. Late in the streak, while absorbing a clean check in a game against Los Angeles, he'd separated his right shoulder. Gretzky—though it was painful to so much as shrug—ignored the injury and kept playing. "I've missed only one game in my pro career," he said. "You've got to play hurt in this league."

He scored two goals and assisted twice in a win over Vancouver to make it 50 straight games. Against New Jersey, he kept the streak alive by scoring a goal early, but the shoulder injury was clearly taking its toll. He muffed a clearing pass late in the game, allowing the lowly Devils to score and earn a tie. Gretzky's biggest fan and most discerning critic, his father, saw the game. "He was there," said Walter Gretzky of his son, "but he wasn't Wayne Gretzky."

The streak ended the following game, and Gretzky was persuaded to finally give his ailing body some rest. He sat out for six games, five of which the Oilers lost. "For a guy used to playing every game and logging a large chunk of ice time," said Gretzky's father, "it was agony."

During this agonizing interlude, Gretzky's desire for a league title increased. His shoulder healed and he retook the ice a healthy man—and hungrier than ever. The blue, white, and orange Edmonton Oilers hurricane rose up again and started whirling, pucks raining down on the goal from every direction. The man known as the Great One aimed the storm at the one thing in hockey that had remained beyond his reach: "I wanted the Stanley Cup so bad I could taste the silver."

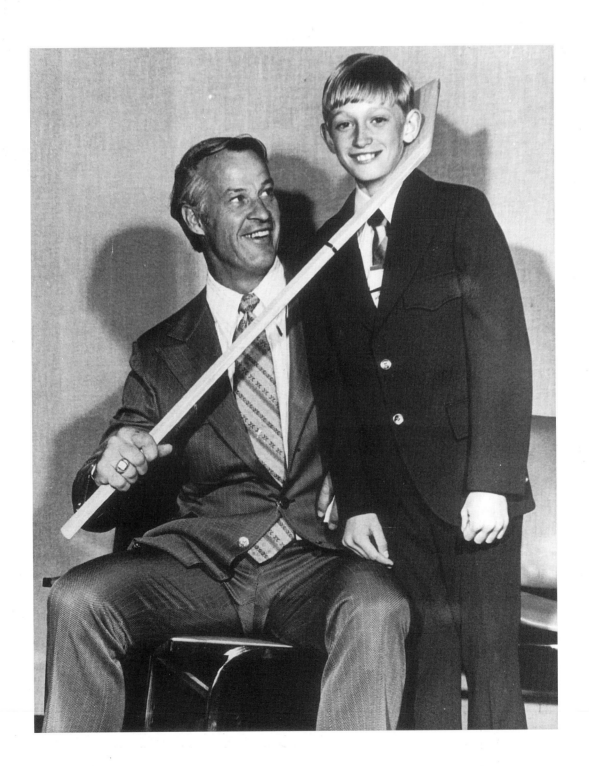

"YOU CAN'T BE NORMAL"

O ften, even during the most frenzied moments of his spectacular career, Wayne Gretzky would make a point of remembering where he came from. He would remember, more specifically, *who* he came from. "My mother and father are tremendous family people," he said. "They dedicated their whole lives to their kids: moral support, financial support. . . . Everything I am today, and everything I have today, I owe to them."

Walter and Phyllis Gretzky raised their family in Brantford, Ontario, a wintry town about an hour northwest of Toronto. Wayne, the oldest of five children, was born on January 26, 1961. He grew up in a modest-sized house on Varadi Avenue in Brantford, but the focal point of his early childhood was the farm about a 20-minute drive away that his grandparents owned. "It was the kind of growing-up place city kids might dream of," said Walter Gretzky. The Nith River,

As a youngster, Wayne was hooked by hockey great Gordie Howe.

which wound its way right through the farm, offered, in the summer, swimming, rafting, fishing, and canoeing. In the winter the river froze and Walter Gretzky, a former minor league hockey player, would lace up his skates and the skates of his young son Wayne.

At the age of two, when most toddlers are still wobbling unsteadily while merely walking, Wayne was gleefully skating across the surface of the frozen Nith. "He couldn't get enough of it," said his father. "You see, once we got him on skates the tough part was getting him off the ice." Many a cold night would find the two Gretzkys at a local outdoor skating park, Wayne darting around on his skates for hours. "Pretty soon," said Walter, describing a typical night at the park, "everybody was gone—everybody but Wayne on the ice and this frozen lump in the car that was me."

Walter decided that the only way he was going to survive his son's enthusiasm for skating was by giving new meaning to the term "home-ice advantage." To allow Wayne the chance to keep skating, and himself the chance to not freeze to death, Walter flooded his own backyard, fashioning a makeshift rink. Almost instantaneously, big games involving practically every kid in the neighborhood ensued. The boys were even able to play into the night, thanks to a bright light strung from a clothesline. The last kid left on the ice was always Wayne. Walter recalled, "Wayne

Wayne's father used to shovel the backyard and create a rink for his prodigy son to practice on.

would even bribe the boy next door a nickel to stay longer so he wouldn't have to come in."

Wayne played all the time, and loved every minute of it. The only rough moment of the day was when he finally came inside to the well-heated house. Then the numb feeling in his cold feet would give way to chilblains. The many-needled stinging sensation would sometimes cause the little boy to cry. "But I don't remember the crying," said Wayne years later. "I remember the hot chocolate, and my Dad's big, strong hands holding my toes to make the cold go away."

Walter Gretzky, after much badgering by his son, agreed to take five-year-old Wayne to open tryouts for a team in Brantford made up almost exclusively of 10-year-olds. Though he was dwarfed by every other boy at the tryouts, he made the team. That year Wayne's precocious skating and puck-handling skills attracted the attention of a local television station. At the end of the year, Wayne showed disappointment that he didn't win any of the awards at his team's year-end banquet. His father took him aside and said, "Wayne, keep practicing and one day you're gonna have so many trophies, we're not gonna have room for them all."

Though Walter could see that Wayne's ability and love for the game promised a lofty future in hockey, he was careful to do all he could to keep Wayne's feet planted on the ground. Wayne rapidly blossomed on the ice, scoring 27 goals in his second year in the Peewee leagues, then scoring 104 goals and 63 assists in 62 games in his third year. One of the biggest newspapers in the country, the *Toronto Globe and Mail*, did a story that year on the eight-year-old sensation. Walter told his son, "Don't get bigheaded on me. No matter how good you are, there's always someone better."

Without Walter's guidance, a child with such astounding abilities might well have begun to develop a certain preening arrogance. But even when, in later years, Wayne was dominating his sport as completely as anyone ever has, he remained a polite, humble, small-town guy, the kind of son Walter Gretzky could be proud of. Walter's guidance proved just as important on the ice. Wayne had a voracious appetite for learning the game of hockey, and Walter, possessing a brilliant hockey mind, was the perfect person to feed that appetite.

Walter stressed the importance of becoming a good stick-handler and an accurate shooter. Wayne mastered these fundamental skills by practicing them for hours on end, slaloming through pylons Walter had laid out across the backyard ice and sending shot after shot at targets set up in the goals.

Such mastery was only a beginning. Walter also gave his son an immense edge in the mental part of the game. "The thing that I drilled into Wayne most was concentration," said Walter. A player, according to Walter, "has to be aware of where everybody is all the time. His mind has to be like a camera." Walter also helped his son see that the quickest way between two points was a straight line: "I always told him, 'Skate to where the puck's going to be, not to where it has been.'" With Walter's help, Wayne was able to begin developing the powers of concentration, awareness, and anticipation that would, soon enough, be catapulting him to the highest peaks of the hockey world.

As a nine-year-old, Wayne amassed 196 goals and 120 assists in 76 games. It was not as if he was producing these astounding numbers against weak competition. Brantford, in fact, was known throughout Canada as a hotbed for hockey talent, producing many players besides Gretzky who would go on to earn paychecks in the pros. Even so, Wayne Gretzky stood alone. As a 10-year-old, during an 82-game season, he scored 378 goals.

By now it seemed all of Canada was watching Walter Gretzky's son. Television crews and newspaper reporters clamored for interviews with Wayne and, almost everywhere he

Wayne set records at all levels of hockey. Here he takes the puck down ice for the Nadrosky Steelers in 1972.

played, huge crowds clogged the stands to get a look at him. It was after suffering a rare loss in front of one of these packed houses that Walter told Wayne, "You can't be like everybody else anymore. You can't be normal." It was not a command. Far from it. Walter was trying to help his son see clearly his unique place in the world. He was not a regular 10-year-old boy. "For you there can never, ever be a bad game again," said Walter. "Every game now, everyone will expect a miracle."

It was unfair for spectators to place such expectations on the slender shoulders of a 10-year-old boy, but, even so, Wayne rarely disappointed. At an international youth league tournament in Quebec City, Wayne shredded a team that featured future NHL star Denis Savard. Savard's coach, Aldo Giampolo, remarked afterwards, "How do you stop a peewee who thinks like a professional?"

At the end of Wayne's 378-goal year, he got to meet his idol, NHL legend Gordie Howe, at an awards banquet. Howe concurred that the spindly, blond-haired kid had a complete game. "You could see it in the Peewees: brains, instinct, desire, love of the game. Gosh," concluded Howe, "I wish I had that talent."

At the banquet, Wayne was mistakenly called to the podium to give a speech. The banquet organizers apparently assumed that anyone who played hockey like a man among boys would be able to deliver a speech to a roomful of adults,

Walter Gretzky shows off some of the trophies Wayne won as a youth.

no matter how young he was. But Wayne froze at the podium, terrified. The ever-classy Howe came to the rescue, saying into the microphone, "When someone has done what this kid has done in the rink, he doesn't have to say anything."

Things changed in Wayne's life after the 378-goal season. "Hockey was no longer just fun," said Wayne. "It became fun mixed with doses of fame and jealousy and ugliness." Wayne was, as the queasy moment at the awards banquet showed, basically a very shy, very quiet kid. But he was increasingly treated like a man, and not just any man, but a marked man. After one game, Wayne needed a police escort to guard him against a pack of teenaged boys (with little brothers on the team Wayne had just beat) who had vowed to beat Wayne up. On another occasion, the coach of a rival baseball team cornered the multi-sport star, saying, "You won't live to see Christmas, Gretzky!"

The worst treatment Wayne got came from jealous parents of other players. The players on Wayne's teams never had problems with the attention and acclaim their friend got, but a small yet vocal minority of parents managed to darken Wayne's otherwise bright childhood years. They hissed and booed him and called him a puck hog. Wayne bravely tried to ignore such ugliness, but occasionally it took its toll. Once, Wayne was found crying in the locker room after a game. "It was what he'd been hearing all game," said a reporter for a Brantford newspaper named Ed O'Leary. "There was no other reason."

"THAT DARN KID HAS FUN"

Even during the most trying times hockey was still a joy for Wayne to play. And he benefited from the support of his exceedingly tight-knit family. His father and mother were always there to guide him and his sister and three brothers were always there to cheer for him. It was his grandmother, however, who provided the most tangible kind of support. During one game, an opposing player named Paul Reinhart (who would go on to play in the NHL) checked Wayne into the boards, pinning him right in front of where Wayne's grandmother sat watching the game. "Next thing I know," Wayne recalled, "Grandma was taking her purse and whapping him over the head as hard as she could, yelling, 'You leave my boy alone!'"

Wayne's grandmother, like everyone else, was powerless to stop jealousy from continuing to rear its ugly head. Things just got worse and worse. "It should have been the best time in his life," said Walter Gretzky, "but he was obvious-

At age 17, Gretzky turned pro.

ly unhappy." The low point came at a tradition-
ally festive annual event at the Maple Leaf Gardens in Toronto known as Brantford Day. It was
a yearly chance for youth league teams from
Brantford to square off against each other on
the ice of the storied NHL arena. But when
Wayne, now 14 years old, skated out to start his
game, a vile sector of the audience, made up
entirely of people from his hometown, showered
the ice with boos. The coach of the team playing Wayne's remarked, it was "the saddest thing
I've ever seen in hockey."

The situation in Brantford had become intol-
erable. "It was so difficult for me just to go to
school," said Wayne. But while the boos from
the sad affair at Maple Leaf Gardens were still
echoing in his mind, Wayne was presented with
a way out. "A phone call came from Heaven," he
said. A friend of the family who coached a hockey team in Toronto offered Wayne a spot on the
team and a place to live. His father and mother,
wary of sending their boy away from home, finally saw that it was the only way Wayne could hope
to be happy.

The rough part about moving to Toronto, which
Wayne came to realize quickly, was that he was
separated from the most important part of his
life—his family. "I was homesick for a year," he
said. But he was also able, in Toronto, to escape
all the pressures and the nastiness that had
haunted him in Brantford. He was able to go to
school without being a marked man and to play
hockey without being booed and jeered. In Toronto he got to feel like a regular, anonymous, ordi-
nary kid. It was a feeling that he fought to keep.
One day a friend of his at school who had no
idea he was a hockey star happened to go to one

of Wayne's games. Wayne scored four goals. "He cornered me the next day," remembered Wayne, "and said, 'That was you, wasn't it!?!' I begged him never to tell anybody, and he never did. Being unknown was too nice to mess up."

After two years of relative anonymity in Toronto, Wayne was drafted by the Sault Sainte Marie Greyhounds of the Ontario Junior A Major Hockey Association. In Canada, Junior A level hockey serves as the final proving ground for young players hoping to make it to the NHL. The top players use it as a launching pad into the pros while the less-talented players, desperate to keep their dreams alive, do whatever they can to distinguish themselves. This usually means they simply try to bash as many other players' heads in as they can.

Into this violent world came Wayne Gretzky, a 16 year-old kid with the frail-looking build of a high school chess champion. In the midst of a season in which he had to be taken to the hospital for X-rays on three different occasions, he said, "Guys are always telling me that the next time I touch the puck, they're going to stuff their sticks down my throat."

The skills learned in the backyard of the house on Varadi Avenue served Gretzky well in this rough league. All the hours slaloming through the pylons Walter had laid down had given Wayne incredible agility on the ice. The players who had vowed to level him usually spent the night careening wildly through the spaces the slippery Gretzky had just vacated. The hours spent learning from Walter how

Gretzky played only three games for the Indiana Racers.

to anticipate the flow of play also helped the Greyhound rookie. He often seemed like he was two steps ahead of everyone else in the league. The head scout for the Sault Sainte Marie team, Fred Litzen, who had been scouting players for 40 years, said, "He's the smartest kid I've ever seen."

The teenaged hockey genius was playing a different game from the rest of the players in Junior A, a different game from anyone, anywhere. To thrilled spectators and to confounded opposing players, his play seemed to be something mysterious, as if he had found a way outside the normal parameters of the game. But Gretzky saw nothing mysterious about it. It could all be explained as completely as a geometry problem. "People talk about skating, puck handling, and shooting," he said, "but the whole sport is angles and caroms, forgetting the straight direction the puck is going, calculating where it will be diverted, factoring in all the interruptions. Basically my whole game is angles."

Gretzky played hockey like a great pool player plays pool, with the vital difference being that a pool player does not have a 6'5" brute from northern Saskatchewan careening straight at him at 20 miles an hour; and he has more than a sliver of time and space to see the whole play and to make the right move. Gretzky's magic—being able to instantly make the perfect play while under duress—allowed him to excel at the Junior A level as he had in every other level before it. He engaged Junior A veteran (and future NHL standout) Bobby Smith in a year-long, record-shattering battle for the scoring title, and he packed arenas wherever he played. Harry Wolfe, the radio broadcaster for the Greyhounds, said, "In 25 years in this business I have never seen a kid capture the imagination of the Canadian public like Wayne Gretzky."

Gretzky captured the imagination of the fans via his own fertile imagination. "The thing that makes hockey great," he said, "is the zillions of possibilities in every game." As he played he explored these possibilities, and in doing so he often made the players around him look as life-less and mechanical as robots. Sam Turco, a longtime season ticket holder for the Greyhounds' games, summed up the feeling that many peo-ple got when watching Gretzky improvise and explore, saying, "Trouble with hockey today is nobody has any fun out there on the ice. That darn kid has fun, now, don't he? I been here in this seat 30 years, and he stands alone."

Near the end of his first year on the Grey-hounds, Gretzky's coach was replaced by a new man, Paul Theriault, who did not see that there was any place in hockey for improvisation, let alone fun. He tried to force Gretzky to play a rigid style that ran counter to his every impulse on the ice. "I hated the guy," said Gretzky bluntly. Knowing that to play any more under Theriault would be, as Gretzky said, "like taking one of my skates off," he started looking for a way out. That way out turned out to be a flamboyant multi-millionaire named Nelson Skalbania.

Skalbania owned a team in the short-lived rival league of the NHL, the World Hockey Associa-tion (WHA). Looking to bolster attendance for his franchise, the Indianapolis Racers, Skalbania signed the 17-year-old hockey prodigy to a con-tract that Gretzky himself had drawn up while soaring through the clouds in Skalbania's personal jet plane. It was a fitting way for Gretzky's professional career to begin.

Gretzky was not in Skalbania's employ for long. After only three games Skalbania realized that not even a teenaged wonder could make hockey popular in Indianapolis and he sold Gretzky to another WHA team, the Edmonton Oilers. To replace Gretzky, the Indianapolis Racers signed a young man by the name of Mark Messier—who would soon join Wayne in Edmonton.

The Oilers, especially their coach, Glen Sather, were ecstatic over their new acquisition. "I hate to put this on him," said Sather, "but a player like Gretzky comes along only once every 10 years."

Gretzky, at that time the youngest player in the league (and in any major league, be it hockey, football, baseball, or basketball), played well enough to earn the WHA's rookie-of-the-year award and to gain a spot on a league All-Star team that played a series of exhibition games against a Russian National team. On that team Gretzky played on a line with a 50-year-old right-winger from the Hartford Whalers named Gordie Howe.

The thrill of getting to play with his boyhood idol was matched a few months later for Gretzky when the Oilers escaped the crumbling WHA for the league Gretzky had always dreamed of playing in, the NHL. Only three other WHA teams were allowed to join the NHL.

Gretzky was downright giddy on the eve of his NHL debut, but waiting for Gretzky in the storied league were scores of players and coaches skeptical of Gretzky's lofty reputation. New York Islanders general manager Bill Torrey remembered the sentiment permeating the league regarding Gretzky as the 1979-80 season was about to begin, saying, "Everybody said, 'He's scrawny; he'll never tear up the league the way he did the WHA.'"

TEARING UP THE LEAGUE

All through the early years of his hockey career, Wayne Gretzky had to battle against players who were considerably older and bigger than he was. As a 14-year-old in Toronto, Gretzky discovered he could avoid getting knocked around by players up to six years his senior by venturing behind the opposition's goal. By the time he was 18 the space behind the enemy net had become for Gretzky a place to begin his assault on the NHL. Coach Scotty Bowman of the Buffalo Sabres remarked, "He's the only player I've ever seen who can consistently center the puck from there through three sets of skates—and softly."

His feathery passes, launched not only from behind the net but also from practically everywhere else on the ice, helped Gretzky lead the NHL in assists in 1979-80. He also became the youngest NHL player ever to score over 50 goals in a season and he tied Marcel Dionne of the

Gretzky won Rookie of the Year honors in his first season with the Edmonton Oilers.

Kings for the league lead in points scored with 137. He won the Hart Trophy as the league's most valuable player and, in an award that especially pleased his parents, won the Lady Byng Trophy for being the league's most gentlemanly player. A further testament to Gretzky's precocious class and maturity came when he was awarded the Charlie Conacher humanitarian award for the time and money he had generously given to charity work. Gretzky was as good a person off the ice as he was a player on it. "Wayne's temperament is incredible," said his teammate Kevin Lowe. "I've never heard him say a bad word about anybody. And he never misses a personal appearance. He just can't say no."

Gretzky's best friends on the team, 20-year-old defenseman Lowe and 19-year-old center Mark Messier, formed the core of an extremely youthful Edmonton Oilers team. The team struggled through most of their first season in the NHL but fought valiantly before ultimately succumbing to the strong Philadelphia Flyers in the playoffs. Flyer Bobby Clarke, glad to be done with Gretzky and his energetic teammates, said, "The Oilers are going to be heard from for a long, long time."

Further notice of the Oilers' gleaming future came the following spring. Gretzky had outdone himself during the regular season, breaking both Bobby Orr's single-season record for assists with 109 and Phil Esposito's single-season record for points with 164. Still, Montreal Canadiens goalie Richard Sevigny, on the eve of a first-round playoff matchup with the Oilers, predicted that Canadiens star Guy Lafleur would put Gretzky "in his back pocket." Many agreed that the series was a severe mismatch, but in Game 1, played in the

Montreal Forum (where the Canadiens were virtually unbeatable) the Oilers cruised, 6-3. Gretzky assisted on a playoff-record five goals and, allowing himself to crow a little, swooped by Sevigny at game's end, patting his back pocket. The Oilers took the second game 3-1 and then finished the three-game sweep in Edmonton, winning 6-2 as Gretzky scored a hat trick.

In the next round, the defending champion New York Islanders also failed to put Gretzky in

Gretzky celebrates a victory over the Islanders in the 1981 Stanley Cup Finals—but the Islanders had the last laugh, winning the cup for the second straight year.

their back pocket, but they slowed the Oiler's attack enough to grind out a four games to two win. Gretzky got his first sense of what exactly championship hockey entailed. It wasn't anything pretty. "Dave Langevin and [Bryan] Trottier hit me with some shots that were so hard," said Gretzky, "I thought my kids were going to be born dizzy."

The following season, Gretzky smoothly adapted to a change in the way teams defended him. Tired of watching Gretzky pick them apart with his laser-sharp passes from behind their goal, teams began sending a defender in to chase him out of what Gretzky had come to call his "office." The problem with this strategy was that it ushered Gretzky from a bad place—behind the net—to an even worse place—smack dab in front of the net. Gretzky didn't have a hard shot on goal, but he was deadly just the same. Edmonton Oilers practice goalie Floyd Whitney put it best, saying, "If you take your eye off Gretzky, he'll bank it in off your skate, your back, your helmet, your wife. I could hang a nickel in the net, and he'd hit it every time."

Through the first third of the 1981-82 season, Gretzky was on pace to challenge Rocket Richard's hallowed record (matched by Islander Mike Bossy the previous year) of scoring 50 goals in 50 games. Gretzky was messing with goalies' minds, and not only by way of his accurate shot. "I do like to do one thing to goaltenders," said Gretzky. "I like to wait them to death. I refuse to panic. Hold the puck, hold it longer; hold it some more. That drives 'em into a frenzy. They can't help but guess you're about to shoot it and lean a little one way and that puts them off balance and, flick, you go the other way, just like my dad always taught me."

After 34 games, Gretzky had 35 goals. Any other player in the history of the game would have considered it the goal-scoring roll of a lifetime. Gretzky was just warming up. "Just before the All-Star break, all heaven broke loose," he said. "Pucks just started going into the net on their own. I'd tip 'em in, bounce 'em in, wobble 'em in, elbow 'em in, wish 'em in." He completed a four-game, 10-goal stretch by pumping in four goals (two of them shorthanded) against the Los Angeles Kings. His teammates, among others, were astounded. "He'll do some totally incredible thing and you think, 'O.K., that's it; I'll never see the likes of that again,'" said Mark Messier. "Then, damn, he does something even more incredible."

Messier's point would be proven in the game following Gretzky's four-goal outburst against the Kings. Gretzky got things started in the first period of the game against Philadelphia by banking a shot in off the leg of Flyers goalie Pete Peeters. By the end of the second period Gretzky had three goals, leaving him just two shy of 50 for the season. A power play goal early in the third period gave him 49, and with two seconds left in the game he potted an empty-net goal for his fiftieth in just 39 games. No one has ever duplicated this feat.

Years later, Peeters would say, "Wayne got what, five that night? Believe me, it could have been nine or 10. I have vivid memories of coming out, challenging him, stopping him. And he hit at least three pipes. I can still hear them ringing."

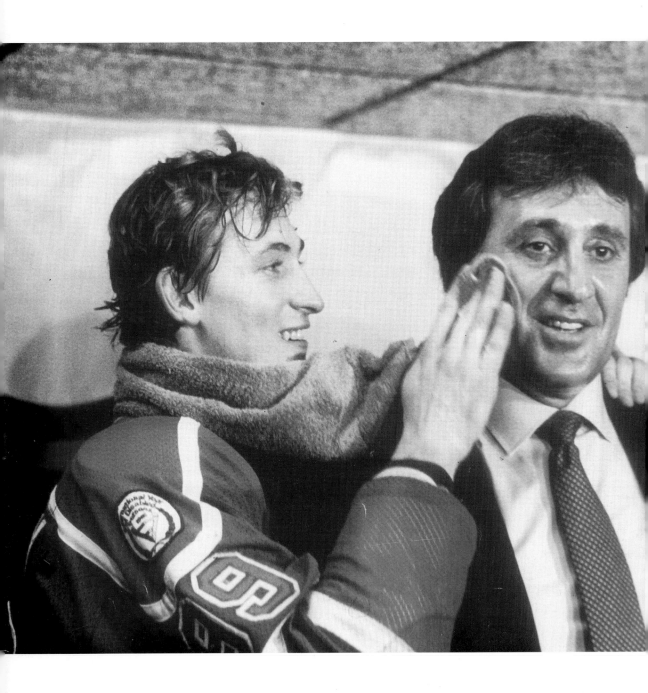

A TEAM ON THE RISE

Walter Gretzky spent that night listening to updates of the game on the radio. About 40 minutes after receiving the news that his son had shattered the Richard-Bossy record, Walter heard the phone ring. It was Wayne. "Did you hear?" he said.

"Yeah, how come it took you so long?" cracked Walter.

The phone call meant a lot to the elder Gretzky. "There he was, surrounded by TV cameras, microphones, magazine and newspaper men, and he'd excused himself for a minute so he could phone home," said Walter. "It might sound corny, but the record seemed small compared to that call."

Back in Philadelphia, one man made his way through the media circus surrounding the record-breaking Oilers center. It was Flyers cap-

Gretzky wipes sweat from Phil Esposito's brow. Esposito had followed Gretzky around the country, waiting for Wayne to beat his single-season scoring record.

37

tain Bobby Clarke, one of the toughest competitors the league had ever known. He felt the need to get something off his chest. Once face-to-face with Gretzky in the Oilers locker room he simply said, "I know everything's been written about you. I think none of it is adequate."

And Wayne had his eyes on smashing yet another record.

In 1971, Boston Bruins center Phil Esposito had set an NHL record for goals scored in a single season with 76. In game 66 of the 1981-82 season that record drew its final breath as a puck skittered across the Buffalo Sabres blue line. Wayne Gretzky pounced on the loose puck and attacked the enemy net, beating Sabres goalie Don Edwards with a low wrist shot on the stick side for his 77th goal of the year.

Gretzky finished the year with 92 goals while also breaking his own single-season record for assists and becoming the first man in NHL history to score over 200 points in a season. It was the greatest single-season performance in NHL history, and it was sweetened for Gretzky by the fact that, for the first time since joining the NHL, the Edmonton Oilers were winning. They steamed into the playoffs with the second-best record in the league. "We went through the bad times together, grew up together, lost together," said Gretzky. "Now's our turn to win together."

Gretzky and his youthful teammates found they still had something to learn about winning in the NHL. In the first round of the playoffs they were ambushed by a Los Angeles Kings team that had won exactly half as many games as the Oilers during the season. Gretzky would, in later years, come to see the stunning loss as "the best thing that could've happened to us. It was a cream pie in the face."

The Oilers came back the following season resolved to shuck their youthful cockiness ("We'd gotten too big for our hockey shorts," said Gretzky) and focus on battling for as long and as hard as it took to get to hockey's Holy Grail, the Stanley Cup. Despite their fold in the playoffs the previous year, it became abundantly clear that the Oilers, once just a one-man team, now had the rapidly maturing teamwide talent to grab the Cup.

Gretzky was joined on the 1982-83 first team NHL All-Stars for the second straight year by left wing Mark Messier. Messier and Gretzky shared a fierce desire to win, and they nearly shared the same birthday (Messier was born eight days earlier than Gretzky). Other than that, it would be difficult to find two hockey players with less in common. While Gretzky moved about the ice as lightly and elusively as a feather in the wind, the strong and blazingly fast Messier powered through the opposition like an army tank miraculously equipped with the engine of a Porsche, inviting the contact that Gretzky so gracefully avoided. As he scored 48 goals in 1982-83, Messier routinely left a trail of toppled opponents scattered across the ice in his wake.

The third weapon in the Oilers' attack (which ended the year with the most goals scored in the history of the league) was 22-year-old defenseman Paul Coffey. Coffey often triggered this attack during moments when the Oilers actually appeared to be on the defensive. "Coffey," said Gretzky, "is the best passer from goal line to red line [the center line] in the history of hockey." Coffey could finish as well as start a rush. In

1982-83 he scored 29 goals for the second straight year, displaying the ability that would eventually make him the all-time leading goal scorer among NHL defensemen.

A pair of high-scoring forwards, Glenn Anderson and Jarri Kurri, further fortified the Oilers' arsenal. Anderson used crafty stick-handling and blistering speed to net his goals, tying Messier for second on the team with 48. Kurri scored 45 largely by virtue of what seemed like a telepathic connection he had with Gretzky. If there was an opening in the defense, no matter how small, Kurri knew to go to it. Almost invariably, the pass from Gretzky would arrive at the opening at the same time as Kurri, and the Finnish-born star would finish the play with a goal.

The Oilers won games with more than just offense. Kevin Lowe, whom Gretzky characterized as a "courageous player," was the perfect hard-working, hard-checking, stay-at-home defenseman to balance the daring forays of his teammates. And acrobatic goalie Grant Fuhr served well as the last line of defense in games that were frequently pushed to a breakneck, end-to-end pace by the fleet Edmonton skaters. Coach Glen Sather said of Fuhr, "I've never seen anyone like him. He never gets rattled or shakes his head or panics." Gretzky simply referred to Fuhr as "the best goaltender who ever lived."

Gretzky had similarly lofty praise for another Oilers teammate, Dave Semenko. "Semenko was far and away the greatest fighter I ever saw," he said. The wild-eyed, hulking Semenko patrolled the ice as Gretzky's linemate, a grisly warning to any opposing player who might harbor ideas about taking a cheap shot at the Oilers' super-

star. If the play against Gretzky got too rough for Semenko's liking he would loosen the strings on his gloves and cruise over to the offender to suggest, "Maybe you and I should go for a canoe ride." A Semenko canoe ride always seemed to conclude at a nearby hospital.

The well-rounded Oilers repeated as Smythe division champions and, more importantly, began demolishing teams in the playoffs. They disposed of Winnipeg in three straight games, then dumped Calgary four games to one. They swept four games from a strong Chicago Blackhawks team to reach the Stanley Cup finals, where the New York Islanders awaited.

In the finals Gretzky and his mates got taken to school. In Game 1, played in Edmonton, the

Gretzky shakes hands with Islanders captain Denis Potvin after New York won its fourth straight Stanley Cup in 1983.

Islanders blanked the Oilers 2-0. The Islanders' impenetrable defense, led by goaltender Billy Smith and defenseman Dennis Potvin, continued to dominate the series in Game 2, the Islanders winning 6-3. In that game Gretzky, held without a goal for the second game in a row, had to leave the ice after a vicious slash to the thigh by Smith.

Gretzky returned for Game 3 at Nassau Coliseum in New York, but the spirit seemed to have been beaten out of him, and out of his team. They lost 5-1 and two nights later lost again, 4-2, to hand the Islanders their fourth straight title. The Oilers, who had soared to the finals averaging six goals a game in the playoffs, had scored a *total* of six goals against the Islanders. Their star Wayne Gretzky hadn't scored any of them.

After the fourth and final game, Gretzky and Kevin Lowe braved a trip past the locker room of the victorious Islanders. Instead of the scene of pure joy that they had expected to see, the Oilers teammates were offered another lesson on what it took to win in the NHL. "Guys were limping around with black eyes and bloody mouths," said Gretzky. "And here we were perfectly fine and healthy."

Gretzky had never been averse to self-sacrifice and hard work. Bobby Orr had once said of him, "He comes to work every night." But it was clear, looking at the Islanders' locker room, that Gretzky and the Oilers hadn't left enough of themselves out on the ice.

Walter Gretzky did not get to see the Islanders' locker room, but he had been at an Oilers practice prior to Game 4 of the finals, and he'd witnessed something that he'd never seen before:

his son dogging it. When Wayne returned to Brantford that summer, the elder Gretzky waited until the time was right to make his point. "We were at my grandmother's house and she was out in the sun working in the garden," recalled Wayne, "and my dad comes up to me and says, 'Look at that. She's 79 and she's still working hard and you're 23 and when you're in the Stanley Cup finals, you won't even practice!'"

Walter's words served as a reminder of what had always been the cardinal rule in the Gretzky household. "You finished what you started," said Walter, succinctly defining the rule. By the time the 1983-84 season began, Wayne knew as well as Walter that there was still some unfinished business with the Islanders.

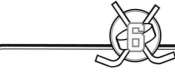

THE CHAMPION

Minutes before the start of the third game of the 1983-84 Stanley Cup finals rematch between the Edmonton Oilers and the New York Islanders, Wayne Gretzky paused to look at the pictures. These pictures, plastered all over the locker room door that led to the ice at Edmonton's Northlands Coliseum, had inspired Gretzky and the Oilers all year long, reminding them exactly what it was they were after. There were pictures of Jean Beliveau and Bobby Orr and Denis Potvin, all NHL superstars, all with their hands on the gleaming Stanley Cup.

In the first two games of the finals, played at Nassau Coliseum, Gretzky's team had been able to escape with a split, but only thanks to the singular efforts of Edmonton goalie Grant Fuhr, who blanked the Islanders for a 1-0 win in Game 1. The prevailing feeling after the games on the Islanders' ice, especially after Game 2, a

Gretzky shows off some of his later awards. He holds the Art Ross trophy, which he won 10 times in his career.

6-1 Islanders rout, was that the grizzled defending champs still knew how to shut down Gretzky and the Oilers.

This galled the Oilers' center tremendously. "Wayne has simply got to be first," said Oilers veteran Lee Fogolin. "With him there's no other way." Gretzky took one last look at the pictures on the door. In one picture, Islander Denis Potvin gripped the Cup as if he was never going to let it go. Gretzky knew, as he took the ice for the pivotal third game, that no one was going to hand his team the Stanley Cup. He and the Oilers would have to forcibly pry it from the Islanders' grasp.

The Islanders forged ahead 2-1 in the second period but were prevented from playing their conservative, lead-guarding game when Mark Messier duped Islanders defenseman Gord Dineen and scored. Then Wayne Gretzky loosened the Islanders' grip on the Cup a little more by engaging Denis Potvin in a corner battle for the puck. Gretzky wrested the puck away from the Islanders behemoth and fed Glenn Anderson for a goal. The tally would stand up as the game-winner and Gretzky, who would end the night still without a goal against the Islanders, would say, "When I'm not scoring I can contribute in other ways."

Gretzky's willingness to muck it up in the corners epitomized the Oilers' effort. They would do whatever they had to do to beat the Islanders, and this was beginning to wear the Islanders down. In Game 4 all the hard work began to pay off and the Oilers, for the first time, began to truly play their game. Gretzky got it started with a breakaway goal in the first period, faking out goalie Billy Smith and scoring with a backhand shot.

From that point on, the Oilers didn't look back. "They're breaking down the great defensive capabilities of the Islanders," said former Islanders captain Ed Westfall. "They're doing it with offensive push and speed. They'll get one guy to make a mistake and somebody has to cover for that man and you get a continuous breakdown compounding itself."

The Oilers outshot the Islanders 38 to 21 on their way to a 7-2 win, Gretzky putting on the finishing touches in the third period with his second breakaway goal.

Before Game 5, Gretzky did something even more unlikely than challenging Denis Potvin for a loose puck in the corner. He made a pregame speech. "I don't think I'd made a speech in my

Rick Tocchet has an Oiler pinned against the boards, but the puck has come free to Gretzky, who is about to lead Edmonton to its first championship.

whole career there," he later recalled. But if the series was stretched beyond Game 5 it would be settled on Islanders ice. The time to seize the Cup was at hand. "I've won a lot of awards in my life," said Gretzky to his rapt audience in the Oilers' locker room. "I've had a lot of personal success. But nothing I've ever done means more than this."

For the second straight game, Gretzky set the tone early by scoring the first goal. Five minutes later, Jarri Kurri shoveled the puck to Gretzky on a three-on-one break and the Oilers' captain beat Billy Smith again. A few minutes later, after another Edmonton score, the Islanders' goalie—once such a menacing, indomitable figure in the eyes of the Oilers—was pulled from the game. As the Edmonton fans roared, Smith skated to the bench, as meek and harmless as a scolded golden retriever. The roar from the stands continued unabated for the remainder of the game, the Oilers controlling play and flying around the ice as if they had wings attached to their skates. When the final horn sounded, the Islanders' dynasty was ended and the Oilers' dynasty had just begun.

Later, in the ecstatic Edmonton locker room, Walter Gretzky forged through the crowd and the spray of champagne to get to his son. "He'd had a lot of big moments in his career, a lot of personal triumphs and awards," said Walter, "but I'd never seen the look of pure joy that was on his face just then—a face streaked with sweat, champagne, and tears."

The joy lasted. During the following season, Gretzky told a reporter, "I enjoy hockey even more now that I can say I'm a champion." This was not good news to the rest of the teams of the league, perhaps hoping that Gretzky would get bored or slacken off on his peerless work habits after finally winning the Cup. That was not going to happen. Said his coach Glen Sather, "He still loves the game and he shows up every day."

The Oilers returned to the finals in 1984-85, this time to face the Philadelphia Flyers, who had compiled the best regular season record in the league. The defending champs came out extremely flat in Game 1 at Philadelphia, and Gretzky was no exception. "Wayne stopped himself," said Sather after the 4-1 loss. The slower Flyers benefited from their extremely choppy home ice and from the failure of Flyers officials to chill the pucks before the game, an underhanded ploy which made the pucks bounce around like Superballs, thus crippling the Oilers' superior puck-handling skills.

Gretzky and the Oilers responded to this like the champions they were. Gretzky gave the team the lead early in Game 2, allowing the Oilers to shift to a conservative, defensive style of hockey. The Flyers were completely stymied, managing only 18 shots on goal for the whole game, only four of those in the final period. In Game 3, in Edmonton, Gretzky further seized control of the series, scoring a hat trick against a Flyers defense that previously had not allowed one all season.

With the score tied 3-3 in the fourth game, Gretzky pushed the Flyers to the brink with a pair of power play goals, the Oilers triumphing 5-3.

The Oilers were now firing on all cylinders. "There isn't a whole lot you can do to stop them when they're at the top of their game," said Flyers captain Dave Poulin. The Oilers went for the

In 1985, Gretzky got to hoist the Stanley Cup for the first time. He would get good at it though, as the Oilers would win the Cup four times during his tenure.

kill in Game 5, wary of returning to the bad ice in Philadelphia, and the game quickly turned into a swirling clinic on up-tempo hockey. The 8-3 romp was highlighted by not one but two amazing Gretzky behind-the-back scoring passes. The dazzling passes served as the perfect exclamation point to an incredible postseason for Gretzky, who broke his own single-season record for assists and points in the playoffs, and who won, for the first time, the Conn Smythe trophy as the most valuable player of the playoffs. (The year before, Mark Messier had won the award.)

Gretzky followed that performance with perhaps his greatest regular season yet, establishing new NHL records for points and assists in a season with 215 and 163, respectively. The Oilers posted the best record in the league but faltered in the playoffs, allowing themselves to get into a seven-game dogfight with their bitter intraprovince rivals, the Calgary Flames. Game 7 turned on a bizarre play in the third period. With the game tied 2-2, Oilers rookie Steve Smith, under pressure deep in his own zone, attempted a cross-ice pass to his teammate Don Jackson. The puck never got to Jackson, instead ricocheting off Grant Fuhr's leg and into the Oilers' goal. Smith made it to the Oilers' bench and then burst into tears. It was the last goal of the game and the last goal of the Oilers' season.

"Everybody wanted to blame Smith," said Gretzky of the loss to the Flames, "but that was a total cop-out." The Oilers' captain knew the whole team, himself included, had lost, and it would take the whole team playing hard and playing together to regain the Cup. In 1986-87 the Oilers again compiled the best record in the league. They then steamrolled to the Stanley Cup finals, winning 12 of 15 games, and continued their hot streak with a Game 1 victory against the Philadelphia Flyers, 4-2.

A win in the second game did not come so easy. After Gretzky scored the first goal of the night the Flyers rallied to take a 2-1 lead. It took a brilliant goal by Glenn Anderson—who blazed past three Philly defenders before beating goalie Ron Hextall—to put the game into overtime. Early in the overtime period, Gretzky gained control of the puck, carried it across the Flyers' blue line, and pulled up, almost daring his opponents to come and try to take the puck away. Gretzky waited, and waited, and waited some more.

A studious observer of Gretzky, Hall-of-Fame goalie Ken Dryden, had once said of this unique aspect of patience in Gretzky's game, "Everybody has a moment of panic, but Gretzky's comes so much later than other players'. When he comes down the ice, there's a point when the defenseman thinks: he's going to commit himself one way or the other now. When that moment passes and Gretzky still hasn't committed, the whole rhythm of the game is upset. The defenseman is unprepared for what might come next. It's not an anticlimax. It's *beyond* the climax. And suddenly a player becomes open who wasn't open before."

The player who came open in overtime of Game 2 of the 1986-87 finals was Paul Coffey. Coffey drew the scrambling defense, passed to a wide-open Jarri Kurri, and Kurri ended the game. The Oilers dropped Game 3 in Philadelphia before taking a commanding three games to one lead behind the play of their captain. "He dominated," said Flyers goalie Ron Hextall after Gretzky's laser passes led to three Oilers scores.

It appeared the Oilers, for the third time in four years, were going to win the Cup in five games. But the resilient Flyers did not comply, battling back from 2-0 deficits in both Game 5 and Game 6 to force a seventh game in the finals for the first time in 16 years. The do-or-die game again turned on a perfect Wayne Gretzky feed. With the score tied 1-1 late in the second period, Gretzky threaded a pass to his hockey soul-mate Jarri Kurri and Kurri squeezed the Stanley Cup-winning shot past a flailing Ron Hextall.

Gretzky wasn't quite done showing off his passing skills. At game's end the Oilers' captain was called to center ice to accept the Stanley Cup. He didn't hold it for long, instead opting once again to make the perfect pass. He passed the Cup to a happy young teammate named Steve Smith.

"THE GAME STILL BRINGS ME JOY"

Mario Lemieux," said Wayne Gretzky, "could snap a puck through a refrigerator door." Gretzky had gotten a long look at Lemieux when the two of them had led Team Canada to victory in the 1987 Canada Cup. Lemieux built on that success in the 1987-88 season by wresting the NHL scoring title away from Gretzky for the first time in eight years.

That same season the Oilers found themselves nudged from their customary position atop the Smythe division. The Oilers had a chance for revenge against the team that ended their six-year reign when they met the Calgary Flames in the second round of the playoffs. Gretzky iced a Game 1 win in Calgary with a breakaway score and won Game 2 in overtime with a shorthanded goal fired from an angle a *Sports Illustrated* writer called "nearly impossible." Gretzky saw the Flames as far and away the toughest chal-

After a tremendous run, the Oilers broke up. Here Gretzky puts a goal in the net past Andy Moog, a former mainstay of the Oilers.

lenge the Oilers would have to face, and he would later say of his overtime goal, "To me, that clinched the Stanley Cup." The Oilers wrapped up the series against the Flames with two wins in Edmonton then blew past the Detroit Red Wings four games to one.

The only question remaining as the Oilers readied to take on the overmatched Boston Bruins in the finals was not *if* the Oilers would win, but *how.* The Oilers, who in previous years had set new standards of excellence with their high-flying offense, bludgeoned the Bruins with a stifling defense, almost as if they simply wanted to prove they could. In Game 1 they held the Bruins to a measly 14 shots on goal and won 2-1. In Game 2, a 4-2 win, Gretzky saved a goal when he kicked a Bruins shot free from the Edmonton crease, then he assisted twice and scored the game-winner on a feed from Esa Tikkanen. The Bruins just got more and more frustrated. "We get no clear three-on-twos or two-on-ones—they always have people back," said Bruins center Steve Kasper.

Game 3 at Boston Garden was another Oilers victory, distinguished from the other two only by virtue of the eerie, ankle-deep mist that hung above the ice, caused by the 80-degree temperature inside the ancient building. Things got even stranger in the next game when, near the end of the second period, the lights failed and the entire arena went dark. Back to Edmonton, and the Oilers polished off the Bruins, 6-3.

Wayne Gretzky, who notched a goal and an assist in the final game to put the finishing touches on another Conn Smythe-winning playoff performance, would characterize the 1987-88 Oilers as "the most talented team I ever played on."

The seemingly boundless promise of this team made what was to come even tougher on Gretzky and the Edmonton fans. On August 8, 1988, a mere two months after the Oilers had won the Cup, Oilers owner Peter Pocklington, trying to dig himself out of a financial hole, dealt Wayne Gretzky to the Los Angeles Kings for a handful of young players and $15 million.

Gretzky was devastated, breaking down and crying at the press conference held to announce his trade. Gretzky's former teammates were perplexed that their boss would let go of the man who had scored or assisted on 48% of the team's goals since they had joined the NHL. The most passionate Oiler, Mark Messier, furious at the loss of his best friend, had to be talked out of holding a press conference at which he would have verbally savaged Pocklington.

In Gretzky's return to Edmonton as a Los Angeles King, a game which was treated as a national event in Canada, Messier put aside his feelings for Gretzky, dumping his old friend on his can with a hard first-period check and winning the game with two late goals. The two All-Star centers met again in the first round of the playoffs. The Oilers appeared on the brink of an easy win, taking a three games to one lead, but, as

Gretzky is somewhat visible —at the top, middle—as his teammates rejoice at his record-setting 802nd goal.

Glen Sather warned his players, "You got a player like Wayne on a club, that club is not going to fold." The warning did no good. Gretzky, fueled by a desire to show Pocklington that he had made a huge error in dealing him, led the Kings all the way back, scoring two goals and assisting on the game-winner in a 6-3 seventh game victory in Los Angeles.

Gretzky made another triumphant return to Edmonton the following fall. The Kings' captain came into the game on October 15, 1989, against the Oilers needing two points to overtake Gordie Howe as the all-time NHL points leader. He tied the record early on with an assist, and then, with 53 seconds left in the game and the Kings down a goal, Gretzky dramatically flipped in a backhand shot to tie the score and take his place at the very pinnacle of his sport. For good measure, Gretzky scored the game-winning goal in overtime. "There is no end to Wayne's brilliance," said an interested spectator named Gordie Howe, adding, "I kissed that record good-bye a long time ago."

That spring, the Kings, for the second year in a row, beat the reigning Stanley Cup champions in the first round of the playoffs. But after the Kings dethroned the Calgary Flames in six games, they ran out of gas. They were dangerous in a short series, but they weren't built for the long haul that was the Stanley Cup playoffs. As they had done the previous year, they went out in the second round without much of a fight.

Bruce McNall, the Kings' owner, was never quite able to surround his captain with the players necessary to win a Stanley Cup. The team often boasted a flashy offensive attack, featuring talented scorers like Luc Robitaille, Tomas

Sandstrom, and Tony Granato, but was all too often undone by spotty defense and inconsistent goaltending. And their captain, for the first time in his career, found himself occasionally suffering through scoring slumps. At one point during the 1991-92 season, Gretzky said, "I never, ever dreamed I could play this bad."

The following season looked almost surely like Gretzky's last. He had a back injury so serious that the doctors treating him knew of no cases in which an athlete with the ailment was able to return to his sport. Speaking of the game that had been his life since he was two years old, Gretzky said, "I was scared by how much I missed it."

Gretzky not only came back from the injury, but he also came back playing better hockey than he had in years. He led the Kings to upset wins over the Calgary Flames and the Vancouver Canucks in the playoffs. In the Campbell Conference final, Gretzky's old Oilers teammate Glenn Anderson scored an overtime goal to give the Toronto Maple Leafs a three games to two lead over the Kings before Gretzky evened the count with an overtime goal of his own. Kings goalie Kelly Hrudy stayed hot in game seven and Gretzky, once again topping the league in playoff scoring, was back in the Stanley Cup finals. There the Kings ran into a brick wall named Patrick Roy. Roy, the goalie for the Montreal Canadiens, proved virtually impenetrable and the Canadiens ended the Kings' Cinderella season in five games.

On March 23, 1994, during a game in L.A. against the Canucks, Gretzky took a pass from Marty McSorley and scored his 802nd career NHL goal, one more than his idol Gordie Howe,

In 1996, Gretzky rejoined Mark Messier with the New York Rangers. Messier moved on to Vancouver in 1997.

and the most in league history. Gretzky was visibly moved by the ceremony honoring his accomplishment. Answering a question on whether this record was the most significant of his many records, he said, "Yes, by far. There is no comparison. I don't think I've ever had a moment when I've felt like this."

Gretzky began to treasure more than ever the moments he was able to spend out on the ice. "The game still brings me joy," he said. Gretzky, at an age when most players had already hung up their skates for good, remained one of the premier players in the game. In 1994, at age 33 and for the tenth time in his career, he won the Art Ross Trophy as the league's leading scorer.

In 1996, it was clear to Gretzky that winning was not a top priority in Los Angeles, so, after spending part of a season with the Saint Louis Blues, he joined the New York Rangers to reunite with the one man who shared his passion for winning. For one season, Wayne Gretzky and Mark Messier were teammates again. Together the old friends brought their overachieving Rangers team into the semifinals in 1997. Fans everywhere thrilled to see that the spark that once powered one of the greatest teams in history could still light it up.

STATISTICS

WAYNE GRETZKY

YEAR	TEAM	REGULAR SEASON				PLAYOFFS			
		GP	G	A	PTS	GP	G	A	PTS
1979-80	EDM	79	51	86	137	3	2	1	3
1980-81	EDM	80	55	**109**	**164**	9	7	14	21
1981-82	EDM	80	**92**	**120**	**212**	5	5	7	12
1982-83	EDM	80	**71**	**125**	**196**	16	12	**26**	**38**
1983-84	EDM	74	**87**	**118**	**205**	19	**13**	**22**	**35**
1984-85	EDM	80	**73**	**135**	**208**	18	**17**	**30**	**47**
1985-86	EDM	80	52	**163**	**215**	10	8	11	19
1986-87	EDM	79	**62**	**121**	**183**	21	5	**29**	**34**
1987-88	EDM	64	40	109	149	19	12	31	**43**
1988-89	LA	78	54	114	168	11	5	17	22
1989-90	LA	73	40	**102**	**142**	7	3	7	10
1990-91	LA	78	41	**122**	**163**	12	4	11	15
1991-92	LA	74	31	90	121	6	2	5	7
1992-93	LA	45	16	49	65	24	15	**25**	**40**
1993-94	LA	81	38	92	**130**	0	0	0	0
1994-95	LA	48	11	37	48	0	0	0	0
1995-96	LA/STL	80	23	79	102	13	2	14	16
1996-97	NYR	82	25	72	97	15	10	10	20
TOTALS		1335	**862**	**1843**	**2705**	208	122	260	382

GP GAMES PLAYED
G GOALS
A ASSISTS
PTS POINTS

BOLD INDICATES LEAGUE-LEADING FIGURES

WAYNE GRETZKY
A CHRONOLOGY

1961   Born January 21 in Brantford, Ontario.

1971   Scores 378 goals in 82 peewee games.

1977   Wins scoring title in Junior A hockey league.

1978   Signs with Indianapolis of WHA; three games later is traded to Edmonton; wins rookie of the year honors.

1979   Wins NHL rookie of the year honors.

1980   Becomes youngest player to score 50 goals in a season.

1981   Breaks record for assists and points.

1982   Scores 50 goals in 39 games; ends season with 92 goals, smashing the former record of 76.

1985   Leads Oilers to second consecutive Stanley Cup; sets record for points and assists in playoffs.

1986   Has best season in NHL history with 215 points.

1988   Leads Oilers to second set of consecutive Stanley Cups; is traded to Los Angeles Kings.

1989   Sets career points mark.

1994   Sets career goals record; wins 10th scoring title.

1996   Is traded to St. Louis Blues; joins New York Rangers at season's end.

SUGGESTIONS FOR FURTHER READING

Gretzky, Wayne, *Wayne Gretzky*. New York: Harper & Row Publishers, 1986.

McGrath, Charles, "Elders on Ice." *New York Times*, March 23, 1997.

Scher, John, "Kings Again." *Sports Illustrated*, November 30, 1992.

Swift, E. M., "A Star Is Reborn." *Sports Illustrated*, May 17, 1993.

ABOUT THE AUTHOR

Josh Wilker has a degree in writing and literature from Johnson State College. He is the author of a history of the Lenape Indian tribe for Chelsea House's Junior Library of American Indians series, plus he has written biographies of Julius Erving for the Basketball Legends series and A. J. Foyt for the Race Car Legends series. He lives in New York City.

INDEX

Anderson, Glenn, 7, 40, 46, 51, 59
Beliveau, Jean, 45
Bossy, Mike, 34, 37
Bowman, Scotty, 31
Clarke, Bobby, 8-9, 32, 37
Coffey, Paul, 7, 39-40, 52
DiMaggio, Joe, 12
Dineen, Gord, 46
Dionne, Marcel, 31
Dryden, Ken, 52
Edwards, Don, 38
Esposito, Phil, 9, 32, 37, 38
Fogolin, Lee, 46
Fuhr, Grant, 40, 45, 51
Giampolo, Aldo, 19
Granato, Tony, 59
Gretzky, Phyllis, 15, 23, 24, 25-26
Gretzky, Walter, 13, 15, 16-19, 20, 23, 24,
   28, 30, 34, 37, 42-43, 47
Gretzky, Wayne
   honors received, 20, 28, 31, 32, 39, 45,
     50, 56, 60
   records set, 11, 26, 32, 35, 37, 57, 60
Hextall, Ron, 51, 52
Howe, Gordie, 15, 20, 28, 58, 60
Hrudy, Kelly, 59
Jackson, Don, 51
Kasper, Steve, 56
Kurri, Jarri, 7, 9, 40, 47, 52
Lafleur, Guy, 32
Langevin, Dave, 34
Lemieux, Mario, 55
Lindstrom, Wally, 12
Litzen, Fred, 26
Liut, Mike, 9
Lowe, Kevin, 32, 40, 42
McNall, Bruce, 58
McSorley, Marty, 60

Messier, Mark, 7, 28, 32, 35, 39, 40, 46, 51,
   57, 60
Moog, Andy, 55
Morrow, Ken, 11
Murray, Troy, 12
Nanne, Lou, 10
O'Leary, Ed, 21
Orr, Bobby, 8, 9, 32, 42, 45
Peeters, Pete, 35
Pocklington, Peter, 57, 58
Potvin, Denis, 41, 45, 46, 47
Poulin, Dave, 49
Reinhart, Paul, 23
Resch, Chico, 9
Richard, Maurice, 9, 34, 37
Robitaille, Luc, 59
Roy, Patrick, 59
Sandstrom, Tomas, 59
Sather, Glenn, 12, 28, 40, 48, 58
Savard, Denis, 19
Semenko, Dave, 40-41
Sevigny, Richard, 32, 33
Sinden, Harry, 10
Skalbania, Nelson, 27-28
Smith, Billy, 41, 42, 46, 47
Smith, Bobby, 26
Smith, Steve, 51, 53
Theriault, Paul, 27
Tikkanen, Esa, 56
Tocchet, Rick, 47
Torrey, Bill, 8, 29
Trottier, Bryan, 34
Turco, Sam, 27
Westfall, Ed, 47
Whitney, Floyd, 34
Wilson, Doug, 12
Wolfe, Harry, 26
Yzerman, Steve, 12

921
GRE

Wilker, Josh.

Wayne Gretzky.

YPVC24128

$15.95

DATE			
FEB 11			
5c			
FE 2			
3LM			
FE 16			
2LM			
4F			
4R			